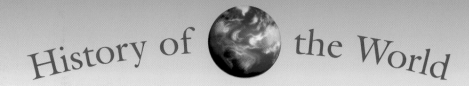

Roman
Mythology

Don Nardo

KIDHAVEN PRESS

THOMSON

GALE

Detroit • New York • San Diego • San Francisco
Boston • New Haven, Conn. • Waterville, Maine
London • Munich

On cover: Hunting Diana, Roman mosaic from Utica, second century A.D.

Library of Congress Cataloging-in-Publication Data

Nardo, Don, 1947–
  Roman Mythology / by Don Nardo.
    p. cm. — (History of the world)
Includes bibliographical references.
Summary: Includes the origins of the Roman race, Roman
gods, the founding of Rome, and a tale of love.
  ISBN 0-7377-1037-3
  1. Mythology, Roman—Juvenile literature. [1. Mythology,
Roman.] I. Title
  BL803 .N37 2002
  398.2'0937—dc21

2001004862

Copyright 2002 by KidHaven Press,
an imprint of The Gale Group
10911 Technology Place, San Diego, CA 92127

Printed in the U.S.A.

Contents

Chapter One

Aeneas Establishes the Roman Race

L ike peoples in all ages and places, the ancient Romans wanted to believe that they were descended from heroic characters. Roman culture was strongly influenced by Greek culture. So the Romans borrowed some of their heroes from popular Greek mythology.

The most famous Greek heroic myth of all was the story of the Trojan War. In this story, a number of early Greek kings banded together in an expedition against the city of Troy (on the northwestern coast of what is now Turkey). After a ten-year siege, they captured and burned the city. Among the leading heroes of the war were the Greeks Achilles and Odysseus, and the Trojans Hector and Aeneas. Later Greeks and Romans held these men in awe. According to legend, they had accomplished deeds of incredible bravery and had actually seen or spoken to the gods.

Greatly impressed by the Trojan War, the Romans created a link between themselves and one of the war's leading characters—the Trojan prince Aeneas. Roman writers told how Aeneas escaped from the burning Troy and journeyed to Italy. There, the story went, he established the noble Roman race. The greatest version of Aeneas's story was *The Aeneid*. The Roman writer Virgil composed this magnificent epic poem in the first century B.C.

Aeneas carries his father from the burning city of Troy.

Messages from Apollo

According to Virgil, after Troy's fall Aeneas and a few other Trojans built some ships and set out into the blue-green waters of the Aegean Sea. The refugees sailed to the tiny island of Delos, in the center of the Aegean. There, they consulted an oracle of Apollo, god of prophecy. (An oracle was a female priest who conveyed a god's words to humans.) The oracle said that the Trojans should seek out the land from which their distant ancestors had originally come.

Apollo, god of prophecy, healing, and music.

Aeneas and his companions had no idea where this ancient motherland might be. Thinking that it might be the island of Crete (southeast of the Greek mainland), Aeneas led his followers there. But after they landed, they received another message from Apollo. This one informed them (in Virgil's words):

> There is a place the Greeks have called Hesperia—the western land—an ancient country powerful in war and rich of soil. . . . The inhabitants call themselves "Italians" after Italus—one of their leaders. There lies your true home.[1]

This is how Aeneas learned that his fate was to establish a new home for his people in Italy.

The Early Adventures

The voyage to faraway Italy proved to be long, difficult, and dangerous. Sailing westward, the Trojans stopped on a small island, slaughtered some cattle, and settled down for a meal; but suddenly a flock of harpies appeared seemingly out of nowhere. These hideous, smelly, birdlike creatures had large sharp claws and women's faces. They descended on the gathering and fouled the food by covering it with their sickening stench. Luckily, though, Aeneas and his followers managed to drive the creatures away.

The travelers continued westward. Soon they came to the shores of Epirus (in northwestern Greece). And there, to their great surprise, they found that the ruler was Helenus—a Trojan and one of Aeneas's kinsmen. Helenus was also gifted with the ability to see into the future. He took Aeneas aside and gave him some guidance. On reaching Italy, he should find and get the advice of a renowned local female priest, the Sibyl.

Thanking Helenus, Aeneas gathered his followers and once more sailed toward the setting sun. Unfortunately, they made the mistake of stopping on an uncharted island to gather food. The island turned out to be inhabited by cyclopes, frightening one-eyed giants. One cyclops, Polyphemus, chased Aeneas and some of his men, hoping to eat them for supper. But the Trojans were able to elude the creature's clutches and sail away.

The travelers next landed on the shore of Sicily, a large island located just south of the Italian peninsula. During this stopover, Aeneas's father, the old and frail Anchises, died. Everyone in the expedition was sad that Anchises had not lived long enough to see Italy, which was so near.

Dido's Love

However, the other Trojans soon found that Italy was not as near as they had hoped. Only a few hours after departing Sicily they encountered a terrible storm. According to Virgil:

> Darkness descended on the deep . . . the air crackled with fire, everywhere death was at the sailor's elbow. . . . The waves towered to the

A fearsome cyclops named Polyphemus prepares to attack Aeneas and his men.

stars; the oars were smashed . . . and a huge mountain of toppling water battered the vessels' beams.[2]

This tempest drove the ships far off course. When the winds subsided, the wet and exhausted travelers found themselves on a beach in North Africa.

The beach was not far from the great city of Carthage. There, the city's beautiful queen, Dido, welcomed the Trojans. She also fell madly in love with Aeneas. Dido begged Aeneas to stay with her and make Carthage, rather than Italy, his new home. The Trojan prince came to care deeply for Dido. And for a while it looked as though he might forget about his fated Italian destiny.

However, mighty Jupiter, king of the gods, did not want Aeneas to settle down in Carthage. Jupiter sent his messenger, the swift-footed Mercury, to Aeneas. "You forget, it seems, your true kingdom, your destiny!" Mercury told the man. "Why do you linger here in north Africa?"[3]

Aeneas enchants Carthage's Queen Dido with tales of his adventures.

Hearing this appeal, Aeneas came to his senses and decided to leave Carthage. Not surprisingly, Dido was both grief stricken and angry. As he departed, she cursed him. Then she took a sword and plunged it into her breast, ending her life.

Landfall in Italy

After leaving Africa, Aeneas and his company sailed back to Sicily. Then, they crossed to Italy, making landfall near Cumae, on the southwest coast. This location was no random choice. Indeed, Cumae was the home of the Sibyl, the wisewoman whom Aeneas's kinsman, Helenus, had instructed him to find.

Aeneas made his way to Cumae's impressive Temple of Apollo and met with the Sibyl. She said that the Trojans had done well to make it this far. But their path was still strewn with dangers. She foretold how Aeneas would have to fight a bloody war over the right to marry an Italian bride; and he would have to engage in a fight to the death with a warrior as great as himself.

Before leaving the Sibyl, Aeneas begged her to help him find a way into the Underworld, the realm of the dead. There, he might once more see his beloved father, Anchises. The Sibyl agreed and led him down into the dark depths of the earth. Reaching the Underworld, Aeneas saw many ghosts in the gloomy darkness. One was the spirit of poor Queen Dido, who had loved him so. The man finally found his father, who showed him a miraculous vision. Anchises revealed the long line of noble Romans who would later descend from Aeneas and his children.

The Master Race

After Aeneas made it back to the earth's surface, he traveled northward to the plain of Latium. There he met the local ruler, Latinus. The king offered Aeneas an alliance and the hand of his daughter, Lavinia, in marriage. But Turnus, prince of a neighboring Latin people, the Rutulians, had already asked for Lavinia's hand. Turnus declared war on the Trojans. In this

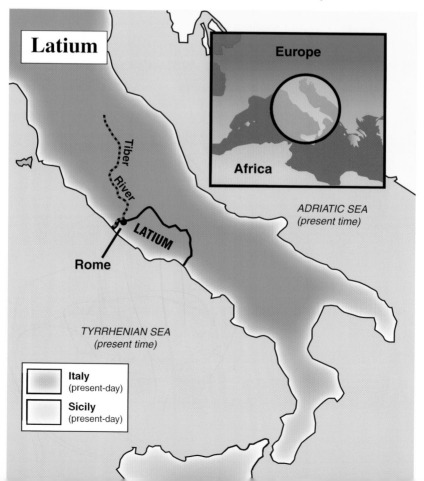

way, the Sibyl's prophecy that Aeneas would have to fight over the right to marry an Italian bride was fulfilled. Eventually, Aeneas challenged Turnus to single combat. That fulfilled the Sibyl's prediction about fighting a great warrior.

Aeneas defeated and killed Turnus, ending the terrible conflict. Then the Trojan leader married Lavinia and established a city, calling it Lavinium after her. Over time, the union of the Trojan and Latin races gave rise to the noble Romans, who would one day rule the known world. For the Romans, Jupiter said, "I see no measure nor date, and I grant them dominion without end . . . the master race, the wearers of the toga. So it is willed!"[4]

Chapter Two

The Founding of Rome

According to Roman legend, Aeneas, founder of the Roman race, had a son—Ascanius. For several years Ascanius lived in Lavinium. This was the city his father had established on Italy's plain of Latium, south of the Tiber River. However, following Aeneas's death, the young man founded his own city nearby. Named Alba Longa, it soon became the principal town of the region.

But Alba Longa was not fated to be the home of the noble Romans. After many generations, the royal house of Alba Longa would produce a young man named Romulus. The gods had willed that he would establish Rome and become its first king. Several ancient writers told Romulus's story. Perhaps the most famous version is the great *History of Rome from Its Foundation,* by the Roman historian Livy. The Greek writer Plutarch's biography of Romulus also contains valuable information about Rome's founder.

The infants Romulus and Remus are discovered by two shepherds.

The Twins of Alba Longa

According to Livy, Romulus and his twin brother Remus were the grandchildren of Numitor, a king of Alba Longa. When they were still infants, their great-uncle, Amulius, stole the throne. The mean-spirited Amulius ordered the babies to be drowned in the Tiber. But they fortunately survived and washed ashore. There, a female wolf found and fed them; and later, some poor shepherds took the boys in and raised them.

When the brothers grew to manhood, they learned their true identities. Wasting no time, they returned to Alba Longa and overthrew Amulius. Then they restored their grandfather, Numitor, to his throne. Numitor asked Romulus and Remus to stay and live with him. But they were young and restless.

An ancient bronze sculpture depicts a wolf suckling the infants Romulus and Remus.

So they set out to establish a new city of their own on the northern edge of the Latium plain.

As it turned out, however, Romulus ended up founding the city by himself. He and Remus got into a fight and Romulus slew his brother. In Livy's words:

> Unhappily, the brothers' plans for the future were marred by . . . jealousy and ambition. A disgraceful quarrel arose from a matter in itself trivial [unimportant]. . . . Angry words ensued, followed all too soon by blows, and in the course of the fray Remus was killed.[5]

After his anger had subsided, Romulus deeply regretted killing his brother. He gave Remus a proper burial.

Constructing the New City

Romulus then went ahead with the plan to erect a new city. He called it Rome, after himself. Realizing that he needed help, he sent for workers and advisers from nearby Etruria (homeland of a people called the Etruscans). They instructed him in the proper steps of constructing a city. First, Plutarch wrote:

> They dug a round trench. . . . Making this trench their center, they laid out the boundary of the city in a circle round it. Then the founder fitted to a plow a metal plowshare [blade], and, yoking together a bull and a cow, drove himself a deep line or furrow round the boundary.[6]

Using this line in the dirt as a guide, Romulus and the others laid out the city's outer defensive wall. The

Romulus shows his workers how to mark the position of Rome's defensive walls.

date was April 21, 753 B.C. Later generations of Romans would come to see that day as the birthday of their nation.

Once he had established Rome, Romulus had to deal with some important legal and social matters. According to Livy:

> He summoned his subjects and gave them laws, without which the creation of a unified people and government would not have been possible. . . . Meanwhile Rome was growing. . . . To help fill his big new town, [Romulus made it a] . . . refuge for all the outcasts from the neighboring peoples; some free, some slaves, and all of them wanting nothing more than a fresh start.

Rome grew into a city of splendor.

That mob was the first real addition to the city's strength, the first step toward her future greatness.[7]

The Sabine Women

Romulus saw that most of those who first settled in the city were men; and they had difficulty obtaining brides. To solve this problem, the founder came up with a daring plan. The inhabitants of several neighboring towns were members of a Latin tribe called the Sabines. Romulus invited the Sabines to a great religious festival. He promised that there would be athletic games, music, and plays.

However, Romulus's real intention was not to foster friendship. Instead, he plotted to steal the Sabine women. "On the appointed day," Livy wrote,

> crowds flocked to Rome, partly, no doubt, out of sheer curiosity to see the new town. . . . All the Sabines were there . . . with their wives and children. . . . Then the great moment came; the show began, and nobody had eyes or thought for anything else. This was the Romans' opportunity. At a given signal, all the able-bodied men burst through the crowd and seized the young women.[8]

This violent act turned the happy festival into a screaming riot. The young women's unfortunate parents managed to escape; and as they ran for home they bitterly cursed Romulus and his followers.

A seventeenth-century painting depicts the kidnap of the Sabine women.

Meanwhile, the girls themselves were quite naturally terrified. They feared they would be raped and then killed. But Romulus assured the young women that they would be well treated. Calmly, he told them that they were to be brides for the Roman men. And he tried to convince them to accept their new situation.

Rome's First Conquest

The male Sabines were not about to accept the theft of their women, however. They gathered their weapons, marched on Rome, and assaulted the city in full force. Romulus and his troops managed to beat back the first several waves of attackers. But the

Sabines of the city of Cures, led by their king, Titus Tatius, were able to surround Rome. A bloody battle occurred directly outside the city's walls and many on both sides were killed.

As the fighting continued, the former Sabine women watched in horror from the tops of the walls. Finally, they could no longer simply stand by and see their fathers, brothers, and husbands slaughter one another. The women rushed out through the main gate and stood between the two armies. There must be a truce, they demanded.

In a famous painting by Jacques Louis David, the Sabine women demand a truce.

After giving it some thought, the men agreed. The result was a treaty with great significance for the future. The Romans and Sabines merged as one people, with Romulus and Titus Tatius as joint rulers. Rome had made its first conquest and for the first time absorbed a foreign people. In the centuries to come, many other peoples would follow this same path. Rome's spectacular rise to greatness had begun.

Three Brave Roman Patriots

Roman myth-tellers had two main sources of inspiration. One was Greek mythology. Because the Romans eagerly absorbed Greek culture, they also adopted many Greek gods and myths. The other major source of Roman myths was early Roman history. Roman writers such as Virgil, Livy, and Ovid glorified the city's founding fathers. One example is Virgil's telling of how Aeneas established the Roman race; another is Livy's account of how Romulus founded Rome.

The later Romans also glorified a number of their early military and political leaders. Usually their stories illustrated traditional,

Virgil sits between the goddesses of the arts and learning.

time-honored Roman values. These included honesty, simplicity, hard work, and above all bravery and patriotism. The Romans expected a good citizen to love and defend his or her country without question.

The Three Noble Horatii

Some of the most distinguished of these early Roman patriots were members of a wealthy, noble family—the Horatii. They lived in the bygone era when kings ruled Rome. During the reign of King Tullus Hostilius (who reigned from 673 to 642 B.C., according to tradition), Rome was engaged in a bloody war. The enemy was the city of Alba Longa, in the plain of Latium, lying directly south of Rome. Alba Longa had been founded by Ascanius, son of Aeneas, who had established the Roman race. And for a long time the city had been the most prominent in the region. But as nearby Rome grew in size and power, the Albans felt threatened. Finally the two cities went to war.

In the battles that followed, both the Romans and Albans lost many brave soldiers. King Tullus deeply regretted the loss of so many fine Roman men. And the Alban leader, Mettius Fufetius, mourned for his own fallen comrades. Moreover, both leaders worried about their common enemy—the Etruscans—who lived north of Rome. According to Livy's great history of Rome, Tullus and Mettius called for a temporary truce. In a meeting held between their two armies, Mettius told Tullus:

The Horatii brothers vow to fight to the death.

You know the strength of the Etruscans, who threaten to encircle us. . . . They are strong on land, and at sea very strong indeed. . . . They will be watching us, ready, when we have worn each other out, to attack us both. . . . We should be able to find a better solution [to our differences].[9]

The solution Mettius and Tullus found was to choose three champions from each side. These six men would fight to decide the war's outcome. The three Romans were members of the Horatii family, while the three Albans came from another noble family—the Curiatii. As the armies watched, the six patriots approached one another. "The trumpet blared," Livy wrote. "The brothers drew their swords and . . . advanced into combat. Careless of death or danger, each thought only of his country's fate."[10]

In the furious fighting, two of the Horatii were slain. And the last of the three had to face his three opponents alone. But the lone Roman was ultimately

---

The Horatii and Curiatii battle one another as the two armies look on.

victorious. So the Romans won the war and gained control of Alba Longa. "The cheering ranks of the Roman army welcomed back their champion," said Livy. "Alba was subject now to her Roman mistress."[11]

Brave Horatius at the Bridge

The Etruscans figure prominently in another famous Roman myth about brave soldiers. Shortly after the Romans threw out their last king, in the late sixth century B.C., the Etruscans invaded Roman territory. The Etruscan leader was Lars Porsenna, king of the city of Clusium. "On the approach of the Etruscan army," Livy wrote:

> The Romans abandoned their farms and moved into Rome. . . . In some sections the city walls seemed sufficient protection. In others, the Tiber River was a barrier. The most vulnerable [open to attack] point was the wooden bridge [leading across the river into the city]. The Etruscans would have crossed it . . . had it not been for the courage of one man.[12]

That man was Horatius Cocles, who was on guard at the bridge. He realized that the bridge must be destroyed. That way the enemy could not make it across the river and take the city. He urged his comrades to begin tearing the structure down. Before they could finish, however, the Etruscan army approached the bridge. With no thought for his own safety,

A sixth-century B.C. carving shows Etruscan cavalrymen like those commanded by Lars Porsenna.

Horatius offered to keep the enemy at bay until his companions finished their work. "Proudly he took his stand at the outer edge of the bridge," Livy wrote, and

> prepared himself for combat, one man against an army. The advancing enemy paused in sheer astonishment at such reckless courage. . . . With defiance in his eyes, Horatius . . . challenged one [Etruscan] after another to single combat and mocked them all as the slaves of tyrants.[13]

Finally the bridge was demolished. As the timbers came crashing down, a cheer went up from the Roman side. Meanwhile, brave Horatius plunged into the river with the debris. Luckily, though, he managed to swim to safety. His thankful countrymen heaped praises on him, and later they honored him with a statue in the city's main square.

A Lesson for the Ages

Inspired by the deeds of Horatius and other patriots, still other Romans fought the enemy with distinction. One of these was a woman, an unmarried girl named Cloelia. After his army failed to capture Rome, Lars Porsenna took control of the Janiculum Hill, across the Tiber from the city. The Romans naturally wanted this land back. So their leaders decided to make a deal with Porsenna. In exchange for an Etruscan withdrawal, they gave him several Roman hostages. Among these was Cloelia.

Cloelia, who was as patriotic and daring as any Roman man, saw it as her duty to escape. She immediately hatched a plot to free herself and some of the

Roman soldiers fight to the death in this sixteenth-century painting.

other hostages. They managed to swim back across the river to Rome while enemy troops shot arrows at them. Fortunately, none of these missiles found their mark.

Porsenna naturally demanded that the Romans return the brash Cloelia. To honor the treaty, they did so. But the Etruscan king was greatly impressed with the girl's courage. In Livy's words:

> Porsenna not only protected the brave girl but praised her publicly, and marked his appreciation of her exploit by handing over to her a certain number of hostages, to be chosen by herself. . . . Friendly relations were thus restored.[14]

The Romans themselves later honored Cloelia. They erected a statue of her, as they had for Horatius. She had shown that Roman women could be just as brave and patriotic as Roman men.

Chapter Four

Cupid and Psyche: A Tale of Love

In general, Roman mythology contains fewer love stories than Greek mythology. Nevertheless, some of the Roman ones are well developed, intense, and/or very entertaining. The relationship between Aeneas and Dido in Virgil's *Aeneid* is a prime example. Another is the tale of Cupid and Psyche. The only known ancient source for the myth is *The Golden Ass,* by the second-century A.D. Roman novelist Apuleius. (*The Golden Ass* is the only ancient Latin novel that has survived complete.) It is likely that Apuleius drew on older sources for various parts of the myth; but those sources are now lost.

One of the main characters in the tale is Psyche, whose name means "the soul" in Greek. She was a princess of an unnamed kingdom. The other main character, Cupid, was the Roman version of the

Cupid (left) and Psyche embrace in this eighteenth-century statue.

Greek Eros, god of love. Cupid's mother, Venus, goddess of love, also plays an important role in the story.

Venus's Anger

According to Apuleius, true love overcame Venus's anger in the following manner. A certain city was ruled by a king and queen who had three lovely daughters. The youngest, Psyche, was so strikingly beautiful that people journeyed from far and wide just to gaze at her. In fact, the local residents were so impressed with the maiden that they neglected their usual worship of Venus. Some started offering their prayers to Psyche instead.

Venus soon learned what was happening. "She could not control her irritation," wrote Apuleius.

Venus, goddess of love, rises from the sea in Sandro Botticelli's famous painting.

She tossed her head, let out a deep growl, and spoke to herself: "Here am I, the ancient mother of the universe . . . compelled to share the glory of my majesty with a mortal maiden. . . . This girl, whoever she is, is not going to enjoy . . . the honors that are mine![15]

The angry goddess summoned her handsome son, Cupid, to help her get revenge on Psyche. Venus ordered Cupid to make the girl fall madly in love with the ugliest, meanest man on earth; that way her great beauty would be wasted and her life miserable.

A Voice from the Thin Air

At first, Cupid had every intention of helping his mother. But when he first caught sight of Psyche, his heart melted with love for her. He could not bear the thought of harming her. So the fate he arranged for the maiden was not exactly what Venus had wanted.

Time passed, and Psyche's two sisters each married a wealthy king. But strangely, no man asked to marry Psyche. Her parents became so confused and disturbed that they consulted a female priest of the god Apollo. They had no idea that Apollo was helping Cupid keep Psyche from marrying a human. Through the priestess, Apollo said that Psyche should be dressed in black and left alone on a mountain. There, a frightening winged serpent would take her for its mate. Fearing to defy the god's will, Psyche's parents obeyed.

Apollo, pictured, ordered Psyche to be left alone on a mountain.

But once the girl was alone on the mountain, no deadly serpent appeared. She found instead a pleasant valley nearby. And in that valley she came on a small but beautiful palace. The building's interior was filled with comfortable furnishings and storerooms filled with jewels and other treasures. Then she heard a voice that seemed to come from the thin air. "All these things are yours," it said. "Once you have freshened up, a royal feast will at once be laid before you."[16] Psyche had no clue who the voice belonged to. But she happily enjoyed the magnificent feast.

The Invisible Lover

That night, as she lay awake in bed, Psyche felt someone climb in and lie beside her. She could not tell who it was because the visitor was invisible in the dark. But she immediately recognized the soothing voice she had heard earlier. In the days and weeks that followed, the two entered into a tender and loving relationship. And finally the invisible lover took Psyche as his wife. All would be well, he said, as long as she made no attempt to try to see what he really looked like.

Soon, however, the lovers found their happy life interrupted. Psyche's sisters came to the mountain looking for her. Her husband warned her not to make contact with them, for they would only bring trouble. But she greeted them anyway. After she showed them her palace and jewels and told them about her invisible husband, they became jealous. They wanted to ruin Psyche's chances for happiness. So they told her that there was something evil about her husband. He must in reality be the hideous serpent that Apollo's female priest had mentioned. Why else would he refuse to show her his true form?

Cupid tries to stay hidden from his lover, Psyche, who has not yet seen his face and form.

Psyche must destroy this creature, they said. She should wait until it fell asleep, then stab it to death with a sharp razor.

Betrayal and Forgiveness

Unfortunately, Psyche believed her sisters. That night, after her husband fell into a deep sleep, she gathered her courage. According to Apuleius, she grasped a razor and shined a lamp on the sleeping form. But there in the lamplight she beheld "Cupid himself, a handsome god lying in a handsome pos-

A statue of Cupid (left) and Psyche shows them touching a butterfly.

ture. Even the lamplight was cheered and brightened on sighting him."[17]

Psyche was overcome with emotion and began kissing Cupid's face. Then he woke up and realized that she had discovered his secret. Angrily, he accused her of betraying his trust and hurried away.

Upset at losing her husband, Psyche searched for him everywhere. Meanwhile, Venus had found out about the secret love affair and marriage. Angrier than ever, the goddess scolded her son. Then she found Psyche, yelled at her, slapped her, and tore her dress. Venus also ordered the frightened girl to perform a series of difficult tasks. The goddess claimed that if Psyche completed these tasks, she would forgive her.

To Venus's surprise, Psyche completed all the tasks. However, Venus still refused to forgive the girl. Psyche might have faced a life of misery had Cupid not come to her rescue. After his anger at her finally stopped, he realized how deeply he loved her. So he forgave her. Then he went to Father Jupiter, ruler of the gods, who agreed to help. Jupiter gathered together all the gods, including Venus, and said:

> Cupid has chosen a girl and made her his wife. Let him keep her and possess her, and as he embraces Psyche may he always enjoy his love. . . . I shall declare the union lawful, and in keeping with the civil law.[18]

Jupiter, leader of the gods, gave his blessing to the union of Cupid and Psyche.

Next, Jupiter ordered that Psyche be given a cup of ambrosia. This magical food made her immortal and one of their number. In this way, Venus's anger turned to delight. And the deep bond between Cupid and Psyche became unbreakable and eternal.

40

Notes

Chapter One: Aneas Establishes the Roman Race

1. Virgil, *The Aeneid*, trans. Patric Dickinson. New York: New American Library, 1961, p. 58.
2. Virgil, *Aeneid*, p. 9.
3. Virgil, *Aeneid*, p. 82.
4. Virgil, *Aeneid*, p. 14.

Chapter Two: The Founding of Rome

5. Livy, *History of Rome from Its Foundation*. Books 1–5 published as *Livy: The Early History of Rome*. trans. Aubrey de Sélincourt. New York: Penguin, 1971, p. 40.
6. Plutarch, *Life of Romulus*, in *Parallel Lives*, published complete as *Lives of the Noble Grecians and Romans*, trans. John Dryden. New York: Random House, 1932, p. 31.
7. Livy, *History of Rome from Its Foundation*, p. 42.
8. Livy, *History of Rome from Its Foundation*, p. 44.

Chapter Three: Three Brave Roman Patriots

9. Livy, *History of Rome from Its Foundation*, p. 58.
10. Livy, *History of Rome from Its Foundation*, p. 60.
11. Livy, *History of Rome from Its Foundation*, p. 61.
12. Livy, *History of Rome from Its Foundation*, p. 115.
13. Livy, *History of Rome from Its Foundation*, p. 116.

14. Livy, *History of Rome from Its Foundation*, p. 120.

Chapter Four: Cupid and Psyche: A Tale of Love

15. Apuleius, *The Golden Ass*, trans. P.G. Walsh. Oxford, England: Oxford University Press, 1994, p. 76.
16. Apuleius, *The Golden Ass*, p. 81.
17. Apuleius, *The Golden Ass*, p. 92.
18. Apuleius, *The Golden Ass*, p. 123.

For Further Exploration

M. Charlotte Craft, *Cupid and Psyche*. New York: William Morrow, 1996. A beautifully illustrated book recounting the charming story of Cupid and Psyche, as originally told by the Roman novelist Apuleius. Highly recommended.

Anthony Marks and Graham Tingay, *The Romans*. London: Usborne Publishing, 1990. An excellent summary of the main aspects of Roman history, life, and arts, supported by hundreds of beautiful and accurate drawings reconstructing Roman times. Aimed at basic readers but highly recommended for anyone interested in Roman civilization.

Anthony Masters, *Roman Myths and Legends*. New York: Peter Bedrick Books, 2000. A worthwhile general overview of some of the basic Roman myths, including the founding of Rome by Romulus.

Geraldine McCaughrean, *Roman Myths*. New York: Margaret McElderry (Macmillan), 2001. An extremely well-written introduction to Roman mythology for young people. The author's prose is enthusiastic and readable.

Don Nardo, *The Greenhaven Encyclopedia of Greek*

and Roman Mythology. San Diego: Greenhaven Press, 2002. A huge collection of short articles about all of the important heroes, kings, gods, and places in ancient Greek and Roman myths. The reading level is junior high school.

Jonathan Rutland, *See Inside a Roman Town.* New York: Barnes & Noble, 1986. A very attractively illustrated introduction to some major concepts of Roman civilization for basic readers.

Judith Simpson, *Ancient Rome.* New York: Time-Life Books, 1997. One of the latest entries in Time-Life's library of picture books about the ancient world, this one is beautifully illustrated with attractive and appropriate photographs and paintings. The general but well-written text is aimed at intermediate young readers.

Index

Picture Credits

About the Author

A historian and award-winning writer, Don Nardo has written or edited numerous books about ancient Greece and Rome for young people of all ages. Among these are *Life in Ancient Athens*, *Greek and Roman Sport*, *Life of a Roman Soldier*, *Games of Ancient Rome*, and *The Greenhaven Encyclopedia of Greek and Roman Mythology*. He lives with his wife, Christine, in Massachusetts.